# Through the Letterbox

# *Through the Letterbox*
## A book of Haiku
## by
## George Bruce

## Illustrated by
## Elizabeth Blackadder

**Collected and edited by Lucina Prestige**
Haiku Music by John Maxwell Geddes

*Renaissance Press*

First Published in 2003
Reprinted 2004
by
Renaissance Press
4 Warriston Cres.
Edinburgh EH3 5LA

ISBN  0-9543961-0-3

Printed by Inglis Allen, Kirkcaldy, Scotland

In Memory of George Bruce
1909 - 2002

**Acknowledgements**

Many thanks are due to John Houston, Iseabail Macleod, David Bruce and Marjorie Inglis, for their help during the preparation of this book.

## Editor's Note

While editing George Bruce's collected poems - *Today Tomorrow: Collected Poems 1933-2000,* I came across a number of haikus absently strewn around his study. About to be discarded - I recognised and rescued them.  From then onwards, George continued to write haikus on every possible occasion and he posted a handwritten copy of each one through my letterbox. They arrived unannounced - each one, seventeen (or thereabouts) syllables of perfection on a scrap of paper, lying behind my front door. I felt privileged to receive them all.

And so I came to collect haikus. The world would be diminished without them, I felt. All humanity is contained within these pages – pain, joy, sorrow, humour, mystery and much wisdom. Each haiku is written just as it was received – some with titles and punctuation, some without, and others in the form of a linked haiku (haikai).  And when artist Elizabeth Blackadder, whose interest took her to Japan (brevity and concentration is also a feature of her work), honoured this book by agreeing to do the illustrations – happiness was complete.

The majority of these haikus were written when George Bruce was in his nineties, some were written in the months preceding his death (July 2002) and have an extraordinary poignancy. Sadly, he died before this book was finished. He was 93 years old and still writing almost to the very end of his life.  He was involved in every stage of this book and I have tried to complete it as he would have wished.  Somebody once said to George Bruce 'George, everything you touch turns to gold.' Perhaps readers will find more than a little fine ore in this book of haiku?

*Blow wind blow through*
*the letter box. It rattles.*
*With a shout here comes Spring*

So here they are, collected for your pleasure.

**Lucina Prestige**

# Contents

# Introduction by George Bruce

## Why Haiku?

In September 1971 I was catapulted, against my reason, into the
haiku form. I had gone to Glasgow to take up the appointment of
Fellow in Creative Writing at Glasgow University, where I discovered
the haiku was an addiction which spread like measles. But where was
the sense in Glasgow students cultivating a courtly, traditional
Japanese form? What possible connection could this have with their
lives?

On my return journey to Edinburgh by train, my mind wandered
to a childhood episode in my Aunty Madge's garden where I saw
growing against a southfacing wall a small cherry tree. Despite
the location, Fraserburgh, on a promontory, north-east Scotland,
they were red and ripe. I stole a cherry. The image turned into my
first haiku. The computer in my brain took over. Every signed
message in one of my books wrote itself out as a haiku – three
lines, seventeen syllables. Finally I rebelled, did not release the
book until I had counted the syllables – 17, of course, then I added
two or three to break the curse. This little book testifies to my
failure. So let the journey begin.

# *Haikus for Humanity*

What is a haiku?
A haiku – a single breath,
that breathes with the river

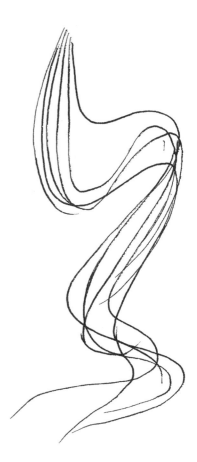

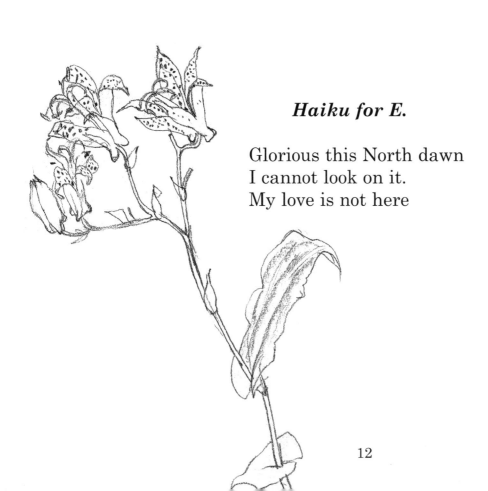

### *Haiku for E.*

Glorious this North dawn
I cannot look on it.
My love is not here

### Two Together

Moon ripens in their eyes
on the silk of water
as two walk as one

### *North Coast Cherries*
*for Elizabeth, my wife*
*three linked haikus*

All around salt in the wind
a mile from the sea
salt on the tongue

Against the wall that
faced south, red cherries
enjoyed by stealing boys

When I think of you
through many winters
cherries ripen in the sun

### *Haiku for Katie*
*on her departure for Canada*

Remember the white rose
of Scotland. Water it
with tears and laughter

### For Rob
*in Canada*

The roots of the Burnet rose
seek out, through rock soil
the water of life

### For James
*in Australia*

Not quite white, near cream,
petals sculpted, formal,
so they touch mind and heart

### Edith

*For Edith Macarthur, actress - on the occasion*
*of 'Robert Henryson and Ballads'*

She silvered the dark
of evening as Cresseid
wept her dark sorrow

***For William Soutar (poet)***

As a bird
the spirit of the poet rises
from the ashes of despair

He who watched time
from his bed for thirteen years
saw green grass grow greener

Bed-fast he stumbled
for breath for thirteen years
then waited for another

which never came but grace,
humanity, and the green
grass grew greener

### *Discovery*

Who am I? Discover!
I am a child
disguised as an old old man

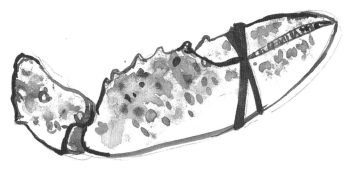

### *Lucina*

Door bolted, windows shuttered
I hear her laughter
in the Spring wind

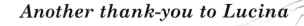

### *Another thank-you to Lucina*

You brought my hidden
self into the light and it
was not at a loss

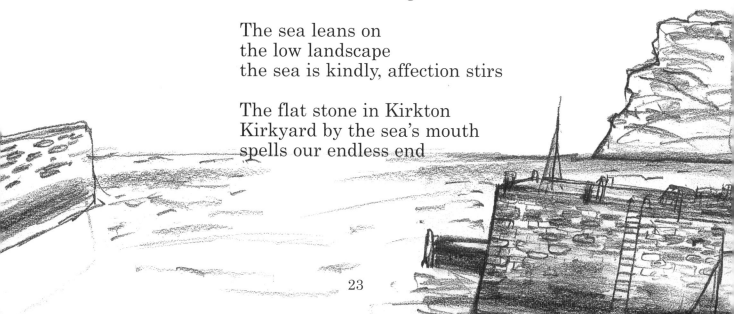

### *Linked Haiku for John Ferguson*
*Rector of Fraserburgh Academy*

Coming home to the sea-town
shared interests
much understanding

The sea leans on
the low landscape
the sea is kindly, affection stirs

The flat stone in Kirkton
Kirkyard by the sea's mouth
spells our endless end

23

### Of Mouse & Marjorie
*Linked haiku dedicated to a mouse*

Sometimes as Marjorie
and Chilton watched television
a mouse joined them

They took no exception
to its company nor mouse
to their presence

24

Friends called. As hostess
Marjorie was embarrassed
by mouse's company

Showed it. TV off.
Gossip with friends.
Hoity toity: hoity toity

He never returned;
felt snubbed at being dubbed
*SECOND CLASS CITIZEN*

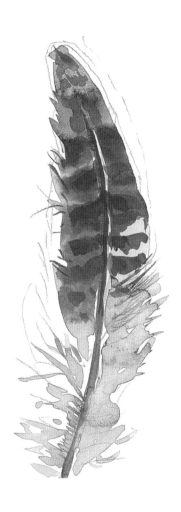

### *On hearing Yehudi Menuhin*

Suddenly but gently,
you stopped time.
There was no before nor after

### January Haiku

*For Elizabeth, my wife*
*Three linked haikus*

She sits in the Arizona sun
snow on low
juniper and dry grass

Do not disturb this moment.
Wind blows, dust rises.
Time takes away space

Sit still in this moment
elected by who knows what.
Now dew beads grass

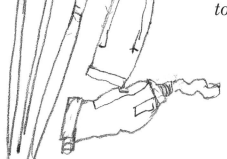

### Colin paints Lucina
*For Colin Dunbar, painter*

Not life's struggle
He looked and saw in her
the happiness of a girl

*A haiku for
Lucina and Colin
to express my pleasure*
                         *George*

28

### *Elizabeth Grace*

She caught the moment
of happiness. A butterfly
flew in the sun

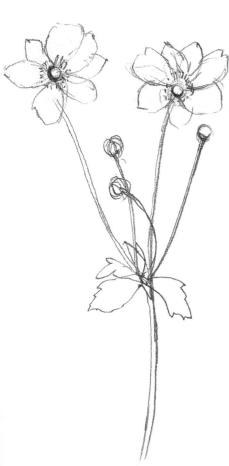

### *In the Garden*

*Grite fule is he, that will not gladly heir*
*Counsal in tyme while it avails him nocht*

In the garden
*Kerria Japonica.*
In the garden – Delight

In the garden
Japanese Wind Flower.
In the garden – Happiness

In the garden
The Preiching of the Swallow.
In the garden – Wisdom

In the garden
Goddess of the moon
Ruler of the Seas – Lucina

### Haiku homage to Robert Burns
### who wrote

*We are na fou, we're nae that fou,*
*but just a drappie in our ee;*
*The cock may craw, the day may daw*
*and ay we'll taste the barley bree!*

'Going for a song' said
the antique dealer
The sage said: 'Plant barley'

The singer sang
to the antique man, 'And
aye we'll taste the barley bree'

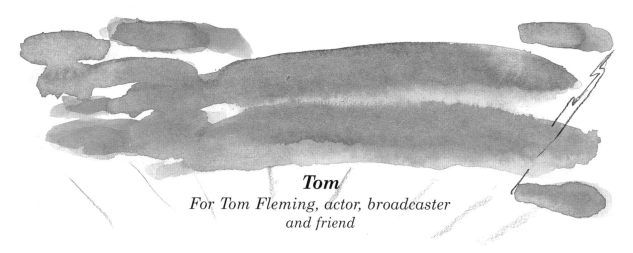

### *Tom*

*For Tom Fleming, actor, broadcaster
and friend*

Thunder and dawn hovered
about us. In that great voice
lament and mirth

### *Hospital Haiku*
#### *for Belinda (nurse)*

The unexpectedness of life –
New Universe
The stars run their course

### *For Heidi*

Dear Heidi, wind blew
Sun shines brightly.
I am lifted up.  Thank you
*G.*

### *For Ian McNab*
*Engineer*

Another journey: another
adds to the quantum
of happiness

### *For Lilian (waitress)*
*at Café Revive, Marks and Spencer*

To prepare for the journey –
Relax, refresh – drink
Then you will revive

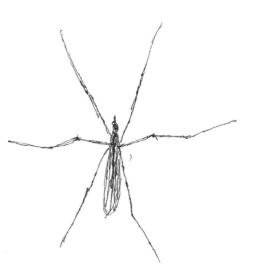

Protective skin saves most
from truth. The Lord Chancellor's
a carapace

# Catspeak

I am taut as a bowstring
Cure me. The sage said:
'Heed how the cat sits'

I observe the cat places
exact foot by foot. She walks
weightless on air

When she lies down her
stretch is as wide as the world;
her yawn engulfs seas

When the planet crumbles
and decays she will stand
monumental, whole

She does not walk. She
moves with sinuous ease.
She glides, is smooth as silk

### *Dialogue with Cat*

'That's not a mouse
it's an elastic band'
'I'm practising' said the cat

### Cat Observation
### watching a poet dress
*(In memory of Scout the cat)*

How tiresome it must be
to have to put on
a new skin every day

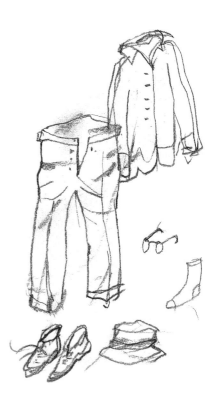

46

### *Four Linked Haikus*

Nor would we have it
other than be with the furies
until they come

Then no thing may be
said. Our words are
at a loss until the child comes

Then this world is seen
in the supreme peace of
the winging butterfly

or the cat asleep
at the fire. She has no dream,
her life is fable

# *Art Haikus*

### *Haiku*
*'Red Cathedral' by Robin Philipson*
*for Henry and Sula*

Not, not the Cathedral
but Philipson's most
delicate hand inspires

### *Two Linked Haikus*
*for Elizabeth Blackadder*
*arising from a visit to her Exhibition*
*at the Talbot Rice Gallery, Edinburgh University*

Bits and pieces on the walls
sail in seas of space.
Peace floats from the walls

Dear Elizabeth the more
I look, the more I look,
*Pax vobiscum*

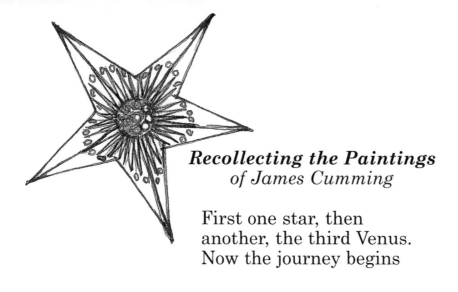

### Recollecting the Paintings
*of James Cumming*

First one star, then
another, the third Venus.
Now the journey begins

### *La Cathédrale Engloutie*
*A painting by James Cumming*

The blue depth of the sea,
the cathedral. 'Peace'
said the hand of the artist

### *Lucina on the Colourists*

All gone but what have
they left behind? Nor
gold, nor silver will buy it

Whisper the word and it
is less than what it was,
so let silence talk

54

'What is purity?' I asked.
The sage said, 'Look at
Mackintosh's tulips'

*Aristotle wrote - 'Art imitates nature – the spirit*
*of nature'. Mackintosh's father grew tulips*

### Sea Woman
*Linked Haiku*
*For John Bellany, artist and friend*

I saw the sun-blaze on the sea.
What shall I do now?
Wait for sun-set

Who was the woman
who carried the sea tale
in her eyes and sang it?

Something of the darkness
of the sea: something of
a brightening day

### The Metamorphic Art
*For John Bellany, artist*

We celebrate the more
because it is taken from us.
This is the wisdom of the waters

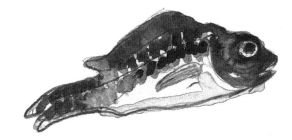

## *Magritte*

In the cage of his ribs he kept
a singing bird
a purring cat

# *High Standing Haikus*

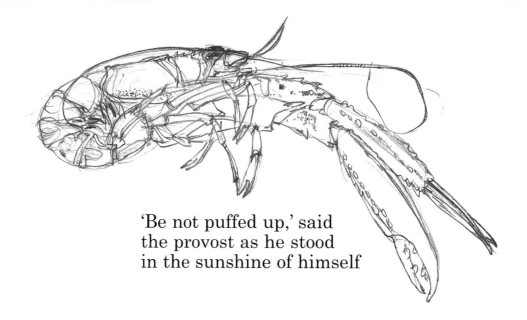

'Be not puffed up,' said
the provost as he stood
in the sunshine of himself

## Shoe Shop

Easy-fit me in that!
This elegance with pain.
I'll wear it, bear it

### *Girl in Shoe Shop*

Comfy bit nae bonny.
Bonny bit nae comfy.
I'll pit up wi it

The C.V. said he was
of good standing. Pity
his knees would not bend

# *Seasonal Haikus*

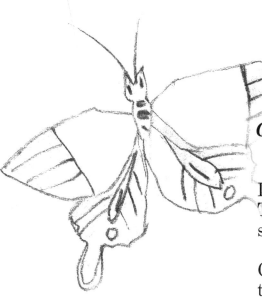

### *Garden at Swallow Cottage*
*For Elizabeth Cumming, artist*

It is the butterfly moment.
The garden is yours
speaks astonishment

Cut out the old: new shoots
thrive. Winter becomes Spring
- the shout of Summer!

### The Silence of the Lambs

Why this Winter face in Spring?
The Master said; 'it is
the year no lambs dance'

*(The year of Foot and Mouth disease)*

### *Castle Haikus*

*Written in response to a postcard of
Castle Coeffin, Isle of Lismore,
Scotland*

Earth to earth, dust
to dust the castle crumbles
The lark sings in the clear air

To make the past a
Springboard to the present.
It leaps a new future

Blow wind blow, through
the letter-box. It rattles
with a shout here comes Spring

Drought-rots: earth will persist
yet still the spirit soars:
Bird of the heart sings!

### Haiku Songs

*'O the oak and the ash*
*and the bonny ivy tree'*
*anon*

Said the red oak
to the green holly tree
'I tell thee a secret

Tis time for my fall.'
Said the holly to the ivy
'Tell one, tell all'

Said the ivy to the elm
(a secret deep)
'I have no fall at all'

I am the evergreen beyond
old, cold winter's call,
Tell one, tell all

Said the gold sycamore
to the green holly tree
'tis time for a fall'

Said the green holly bush
to the ivy on the wall
'we have no fall at all'

It is one of those days
wind and sunshine,
chosen to suggest Heaven

Sun shines, wind blows
Go home. Come out again.
Merrier than before even

### *To Lucina*

Wind-blown. I am
the tatters of time, but
heart is with you already

# *Fishy Haikus*

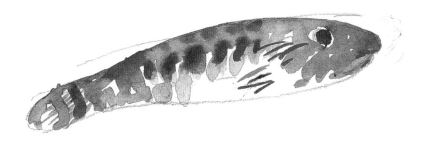

### FISH SHOP OPEN – *9am-1pm*
*(unless no fish)*

See pretty girl
seek her. Go catch her.
Gone fishing

### *No Fish*

'Patience is your virtue?'
Go, wait for tide, bait line,
content: catch no fish

### Haiku Fishy Conversation
*For Malcolm McKay, lawyer*

'Why' said Big-fish 'do I not
lead?' 'Small-fish needs
your company: you ours'

### Haiku for Andrew Noble
*(fisherman)*

This day the sun shines bright
but not as its silver flash
in Fraserburgh

The haven of the *Silver Crest* and no doubt as to assurance

She is touched by the dry
bones of the fish and the world
trembles and bleeds

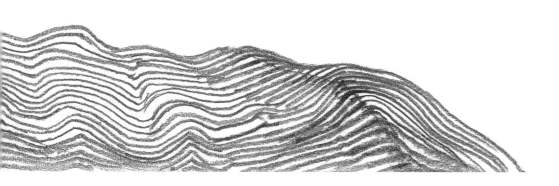

Visitor from the sea,
tell her my lips are ready
for the occasion

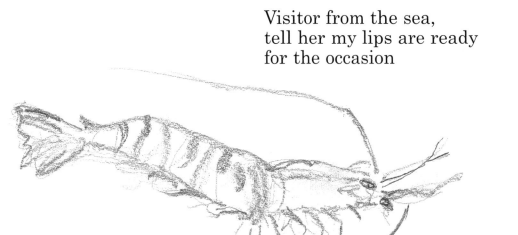

# *Green Pot Haikus*

What does it take to make
a small green pot? The light
touch of timelessness

What does it take to make
a small green pot? Go, study.
Go, study Confucius

What does it take to make
one pot? Let time slip by
without grief or why

Whit wey dae ye mak a sma
green pot? Muckle care
an mair an mair an mair

What are the ingredients?
A sniff of pepper, a touch
of kindness

Once a haiku met a
small green pot - perfection.
They met in heaven

The branch of youth blossomed.
The wisdom of age blossomed.
Heaven was made

Bowl from Earth. Earth man
made it, holds to his self
Water of Life. He drinks

# *Bath Haikus*

### *The Bath*

Not, not, the Roman
Public Baths, nor
the public baths of Portobello

but solo incommunicado,
except with self
or selflessness

Begin, begin with
the anointing, respect
not due for tribal man

88

Possibility of growth
towards human,
not evolution

One progress only,
charity, yet not to
be held in heart, but given

to the meanest, not dearest,
habituée of the hut
in which we all dwell

momentarily. Forever
trusting the other
fragment we are

The waters fall, forgiving,
like raindrops on our
head, eyes, nose, lips

The wholeness is theirs.
We are begun anew
at the breaking of waters

90

not thinking, being as
if light breaks on us for
the first time. Millions

star-distant years are moment
here now. I
stand on a bath mat become

prayer mat, upright, knowing
no word, number, sign,
will tell, be our tale

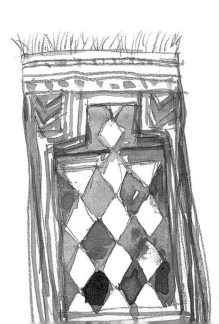

# *Philosophical Haikus*

### *The Right Headgear for*
### *The President of USA*

The President
wears a ten-gallon hat.
Why? In case he hears something

### 25 Warriston Cres.

Night: I come back
to this empty house. My poems
look at me with cold eyes

My desk deep in papers,
unfinished poems. Cut
the rope. Put the boat out

### *A Modest Proposal*

To exercise power engrave
in stone: to show wisdom
write in sand

### *Laughter*

Laughter in the eyes
of the sage. I asked what
it meant. He said laughter

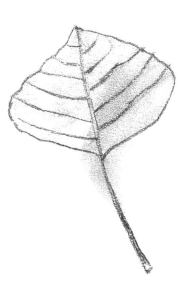

### *Perspective*

The perspective of the haiku
is lean, no fat.
*Multum in parvo*

## *Mist*

Mist shrouds the Firth
allows entry only
to the finger of the mind

### *I am*

Concept of dust, off-load
in space, blind, but for
the iris of the mind

### *Help!*
*Linked haiku*

I went to the sage,
No words said. In his eyes
was written amazement

I asked for help. He said
Help has been given.
Go your way I go mine

## *Morning Star*

Let it be nameless
It is beyond the touch
of utterance and life

### *Venus*

Saftly, saftly lichts
the mornin star. The black
abyss will nae oot it

### *Linked Haiku*

I shall always remember
the candle-lights
on the water-lilies

still, but for their tremble
in a light breeze –
life, precarious, delicate

### *Candles*

'Quick, quick' said the bird,
'the white candles are lit
on the great chestnut tree'

### *Botanic Gardens*

Two pigeons at my feet –
fussy conversation.
Should I interrupt?

### *End Game*

Where all the leaves
have fallen dead from the tree
there is nor dance nor glee

### Objet Trouvé
*Three linked haikus*

Bowl from earth, earth man
made it, holds to his self
water of life. He drinks

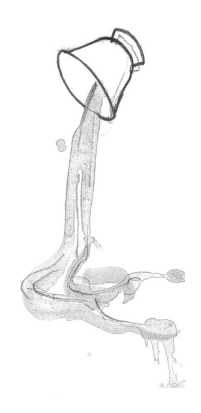

Night. A star looks from
the water. He touches silver.
Star trembles. Gone

Sun rises. He pours
a libation to sun. Earth
drinks. Dust unto dust

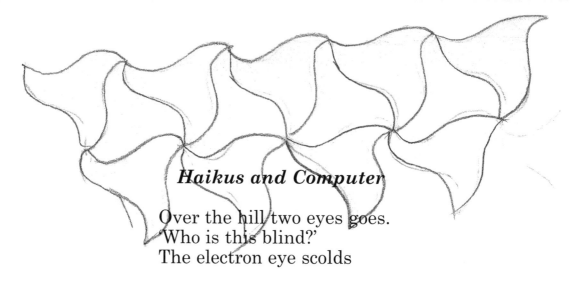

### *Haikus and Computer*

Over the hill two eyes goes.
'Who is this blind?'
The electron eye scolds

'Two-legged homunculi
computered man and me,'
quoth electron eye

I cross two sticks on the shore.
Two crossed sticks make
two thousand years. Miracles

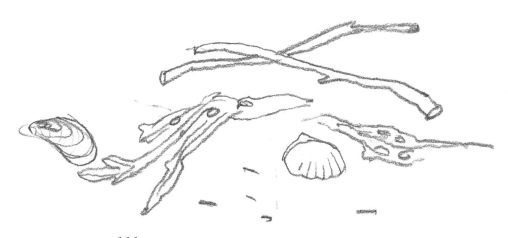

### *Burdens*

'Carry your bags?'
No bags. I journey
carrying the luggage of life

### *Journey Ended*

Journey near ended.
Hat off, shoes off.
Fever of life no more

## *Wisdom and Follies Haikus*

Books – thousands – on shelves –
Wisdom of ages.
Folly if not in me

When two words do
for ten, then there is
the possibility of wisdom

When ten words set out
to do what two will do
then there is foolishness

Draw a line between the
possible and probable on sand
then go swimming

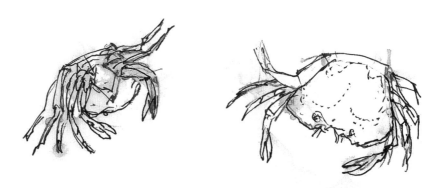

I said to the great violinist,
'You stopped time.'
He put his bow to work again

I dislike this
Quixote in me. Cervantes
said: 'Try Sancho Panza'

### Scots Haiku
*On completion of the*
*Scottish National Dictionary*

Noo a thae words
are in their tomb
whan will be the resurrectioun?

***5am   24 July 1998***

*This dawn I awoke with*

The master said,
'the greatest miracle is
to turn wounds into mercies'

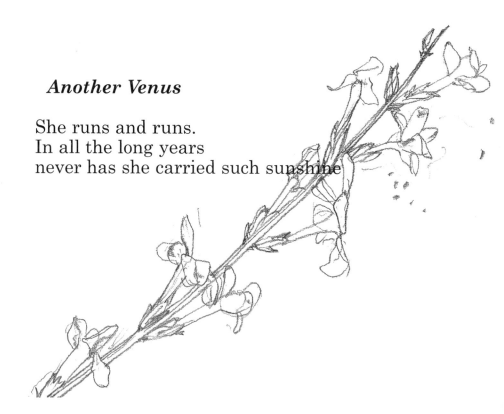

### Another Venus

She runs and runs.
In all the long years
never has she carried such sunshine

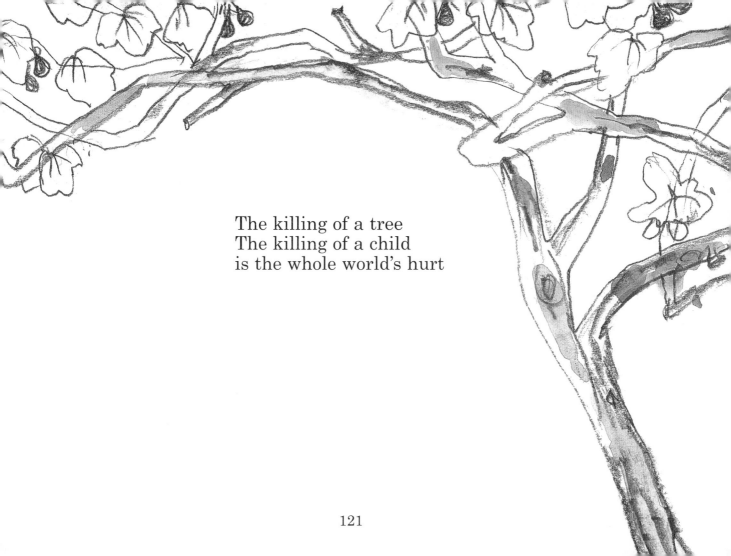

The killing of a tree
The killing of a child
is the whole world's hurt

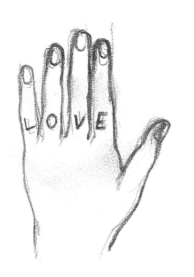

We wounded are at
Address unknown, nameless.
We kept our name-plate, LOVE

The door down, black burnt,
yet on it grief grew a word,
a new name-plate, HATE

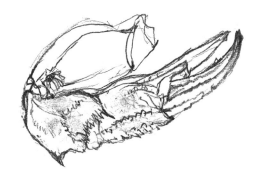

A journey-man poet said:
'Let exultation thrive.
Scarce enough these days'

## *Journeyman*

Journey-man poet: a craftsman
who does the
job on request

### *For Truth's sake*

First know this:
The light is there before me
The light is there after me

### The Sleep of Love

Today the god of love sleeps.
Will he ever awake?
When the blood-letting stops

Look a pot of gold
at this end of a rainbow.
Look again. Not there

Pray give heed to
the round O. It contains
all being. Shakespeare's theatre

Please keep my heart
to the day's end when
I am bound to a grain of wheat

### *Chat in the Firestation Restaurant*
### *Gibson, North Carolina*

He lived 300 years
in Gibson. Sure
it was writ on his tombstone

She said her gran-dad
had shot a black dead.
Why? 'Didn't run fast enough'

Trains go rumble, rumble
through Gibson. Can't hear
a thing. 'Good, good, say trains'

Will the God of Love
rise again? When the heart
is no longer a stone

When goodwill and understanding
walk through the door,
what more is required?

### *On the train*
### *from Aberdeen to Edinburgh*

What is that rare sound?
It is the braying of asses,
that know not why

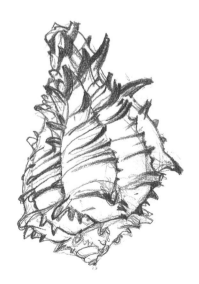

It is not that it is still
but that it presents
the stillness in things

'I have lost my way' the old man
said. Then you have found it.
Ask no more

Such is your kindness, I
would have it with me
until time wore out

I would stare time
in the face. It has none.
Listen. It has a tale to tell

Night. A star looks from
the water. He touches silver.
Star trembles. Gone

Sun rises. Earth drinks
A libation to the sun
Dust unto dust

### *Endless haiku*

What is the question?
The question cannot be answered
without another question - peace

For a moment sun and sea
stopped together. What next?
Wait for the sunset

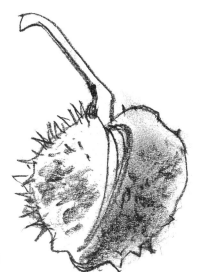

You are in doubt about
the meaning of usury.
Scrub the cupboard clean

Let the word-horse decide
its pace. If right
the rhythm of life is yours

Let the work-horse canter,
no gallop. If the pace be true,
be right, go your way

The wild trade in hope
locks me to this life
I cannot, will not, let it go

Yet this is the delicate matter
of spirit. A wind blows
I live in the breath

Aches of the unsteady
universe are ours.
Love life, still it blesses

## *Living on the Planet*

In his age he waxed
lyrical. He saw the
whole thing was a fable

What's next? Gossip. Gossip.
Say the birds. Words.
Nothing. Wait for a red moon

Haiku wisdom.
Do not attempt to catch the
knife which has dropped from your hand

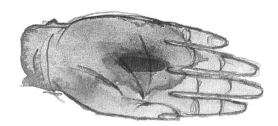

148

She answered out of the dark
womb of time to take
to herself all the world

To build a house you
need stones or wood: to make
a home, the patience of love

What do I do next?
Write a haiku or two or three,
said the Master

Once I have made a thing
it is not my business
to judge its effect

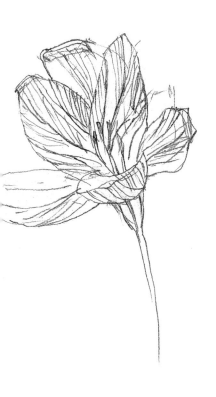

Perhaps, perhaps
a little time is left
for verbal communication

### *Butterfly*

Eccentric in motion -
She arrives at the unquiet sea
Ignorant, nameless

Many miles she carries,
Joy in the ear of the wind,
Rhododendron

The child of life
is light years from
the child demanded by society

156

And so we shall eat our cake
and eat it and then
greet friends at the door

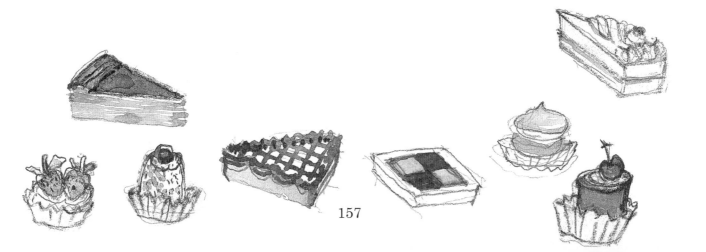

157

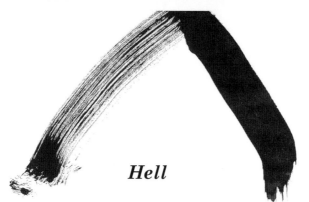

### *Hell*

The transmission of
nothing: option: meeting
an asteroid

He that protests wisdom is his,
is not his. Be hopeful.
Nothing more

### *Flower Postcard*

Perfection is the evanescence
of flowers, but these
do not fade

When shall I know
the answer? As night falls
with double tongue she tells all

At six years clarity
of perception.
At sixty all is clouded

162

It is the silences, pauses
in the poems that matter
more than words

Only when your being is
touched into life
can you believe in existence

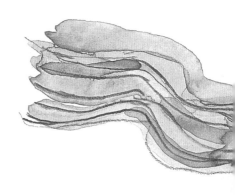

Sae saft, sae saft, the
hinmost o the nicht when a'
thing is gone 'cept sleep

### *Haiku envoi*

The sea trembles - voiceless.
It is the rare moment
when a word is sought

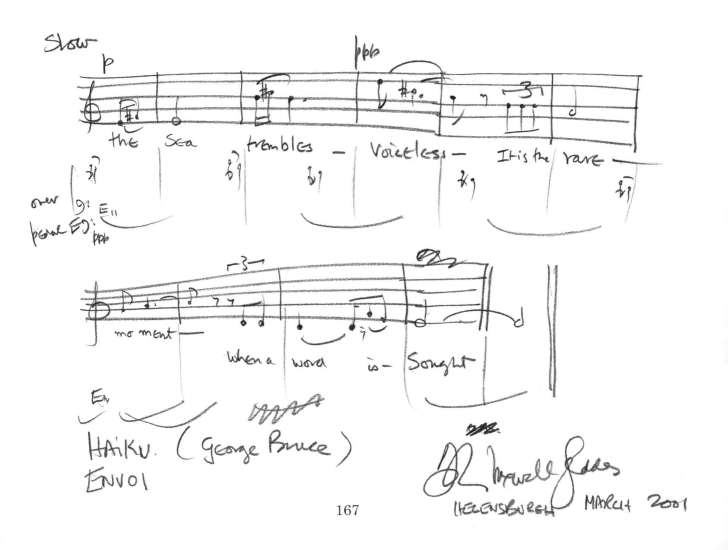

HAIKU. (George Bruce)
ENVOI

167

# Haiku Envoi

*for George Bruce*

George Bruce

John Maxwell Geddes
Helensburgh , March 2001

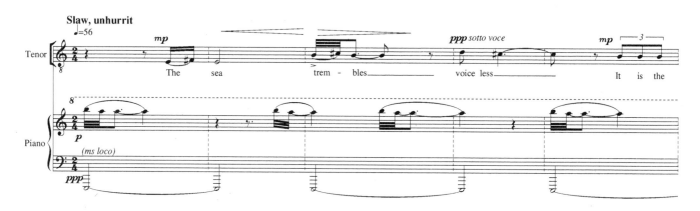

The sea trem - bles_____ voice less_____ It is the

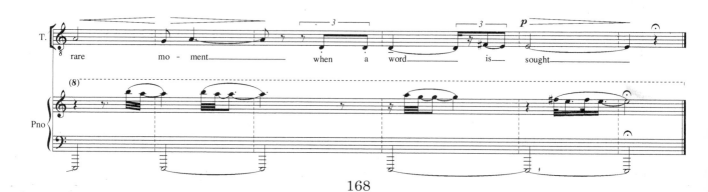

rare mo - ment_____ when a word_____ is_____ sought